The Adult Chair
a guide to loving yourself

Michelle Chalfant

D1534053

This book is dedicated to Susan.

For helping me to integrate my selves and finding wholeness, for giving me the experience of unconditional love, for helping me to sit in my Adult Chair.

I am eternally grateful.

CONTENTS

Are we indeed broken?

Or do we simply not know who we really are?

INTRODUCTION

"Oh wait, I'm in the Adult Chair now!", exclaimed one of my clients excitedly as she quickly jumped up from the medium-sized chair in my office to the larger chair.

"I get it. Now I can see what the problem is and how I've been contributing to it."

After years of "traditional" therapy and minimal progress, Wendy had almost given up on ever finding her way out of the emotional storm that was ruining her life. Yet here she was, beaming at me as she explained that she felt as if someone had just pulled back a curtain to reveal the true nature of her problem and some of its inherent solutions. In this first session with me, Wendy had finally stepped out of her emotional suffering and she was beyond thrilled.

I have seen thousands of clients during the 20 years I have been in private practice as a psychotherapist and coach. We have worked on a wide range of issues ranging from depression and anxiety to codependency and relationship problems with spouses and children, from weight loss and body hatred to job and money struggles. And during all that time, the Adult Chair model has proven to be the most simple and profound way I have found yet to help individuals and couples navigate the world as centered, peaceful, empowered people. Of course, it is not a magic bullet. But I can confidently say that it is the most effective way to clear out the mess in your mind and help guide you on your journey through all of life's obstacles and challenges.

How can I say this with such confidence?

I have always wanted to help people face the storm clouds and headwinds that make life much harder than it needs to be with speed and relative ease. When I began my career, I knew that I didn't want to build a practice using traditional counseling and psychotherapy methods. It didn't make sense to me that my clients needed to see me every week for years and years to achieve small improvements. There had to be a better way and I was determined I would find it.

I have spent most of my 20 plus years in practice searching for new, different and better ways to help people. I've tested the best with actual clients. Some of the approaches and models were just different twists on tradition, while others (like energy medicine, meditation, Neuro-Linguistic Programming and acupressure) were a bit more "radical". The ones that really worked became part of my unique practice, and my clients have benefitted by experiencing much better results in much shorter time frames.

Every teacher needs a teacher, a wise mentor they can learn from. That's why I've always taken classes—to learn from the best. In 2012, I began an intensive program in Nashville that was run by an amazing woman named Susan Austin-Crumpton. Over the four years I studied with her, I saw my own life improve in dramatic ways. It was Susan who introduced me to a unique experiential approach to therapy that she called the Adult Chair. With Susan's blessing, I made this approach the basis for my work with clients and integrated my other teachings, approaches and tools into the *Adult Chair Model*. She has encouraged me to share this valuable approach. I have done this through podcasts, books, videos and lectures, as well as through my counseling practice.

As more and more of my clients experience the Adult Chair, more and more of them have been asking me to write a book for them to use when they're not in my office — something easy-to-read that they could share with their family and friends. This introductory guidebook is for all of them — and for you. Use it to begin to uncover the underlying problems that make life more of a struggle than an adventure and to begin to discover the "real" you.

I hope that you enjoy reading this book and that, when you use it, you experience the power of "sitting" in your Adult Chair more often each day.

May this method for understanding and loving yourself bring you as much peace and happiness as it has brought me and my clients.

xo,

Michelle Chalfant
December 2016
Nashville, TN

What is The Adult Chair

"When I was a child, I talked like a child, I thought like a child, I reasoned like a child. When I became a man, I set aside childish ways."

Berean Bible
1 Corinthians 13:11

When you come into my office, you'll see three different chairs. The smallest one represents the "inner child", the medium chair represents the adolescent and the largest is for the adult. As you begin to explain what you're going through at the moment, I'll have you move to a chair that corresponds with the perspective you're taking.

This is usually the big light bulb moment for most people.

We all think we're adults all of the time. But as you start shifting back and forth between the three chairs, you'll quickly realize, just like all my clients do, that we may look and dress like adults, but we still act and re-act to life using maps and strategies from our childhood and adolescence. Many of my clients are surprised to find that most people find themselves spending more than 90% of their time sitting in their Adolescent Chair. When here, we make decisions while stuck with emotions equivalent to those of a 12-year-old.

The Adult Chair is where we really want to stay. Think of this chair as a metaphor for where we "sit" (or exist) when we are acting and speaking from the highest version, the most healed version of ourselves. In a nutshell, it's where we live when we are authentic.

Why do so few of us sit continuously in this place? Perhaps that's because we believe that living from the highest version of ourselves is a special experience, reserved for only a very few. After all, this is somewhere we might get to after years of meditation and reflection. The path will be very hard and it will take a very long time.

I don't believe it is.

The Adult Chair is a ground-breaking shortcut on this path to self-realization and authentic living. What I have found is that when we learn who we are at our deepest level, how to feel our emotions, what our triggers are and why we react the way we do, we then begin to find compassion for ourselves. Self-compassion opens the door: we begin to like ourselves and be easy on ourselves for our mistakes. Feelings of self-love begin to seep in and we start to operate from a "higher place" (or what I like to call our "higher mind"). We connect with the highest version of ourselves. Our lives change.

I've seen this with my clients as they work with the Adult Chair model. They discover how to identify the different parts of themselves and what drives those parts to protect them and keep them safe. They quickly realize that, no, they are not "broken" or "bad", unlovable or unhealable. They have just misunderstood who they are. All they have to do is take a deeper look at themselves to see that who they are is actually okay.

When you start to work with the three chairs and the different parts of yourself, you too will begin to see the maps, the masks and the triggers that you've been living with. And as you become more and more comfortable sitting in your Adult Chair, you'll find your life begin to fill with self-love, compassion, inner peace and the freedom that comes from just being yourself.

How do we grow from one chair to the next?

Each chair represents one of the three distinct developmental phases we go through in life. Here is how life plays out, in varying degrees, for most everyone as they move through these phases.

As vulnerable, innocent children, we are like little sponges taking everything in around us. Our parents, older siblings and other people mean well, but they pass along confusing, distorted, often damaging messages.

As children, we rely on the adults around us to mirror back to us who we are. Most of the time, instead of a reflection of who we are, we get a projection from our parents of the unhealed wounds that distinguish who they are. Being innocent, we mistakenly believe that our parents' wounds and pain are our own. In all this, we miss out on the important messages we really need to hear about how lovable and amazing we are.

The projections of our parents often feel confusing and make us doubt ourselves. But we get the message loud and clear: we need to bury our vulnerable self, our innocent self, our true self to have a fighting chance of being allowed to stay in the tribe. We have to make every attempt to become lovable to those around us and to, no matter what, avoid rejection. The tribe is, after all, where we will be connected and safe. So we bury our real self behind masks, those disguises we create to help us fit in and which we will eventually put on to become who we think others want us to be.

Throughout this first phase of development, we record everything and store it all in our subconscious and unconscious minds. We learn how to navigate the world. With that learning, we create a map of how the world works, how to show up in it and how to stay safe. In response to our longing to feel lovable and loved just for who we really are, we begin our real search for love.

Around the age of seven, we become aware that we are separate from others. This awakening of our ego marks the beginning of our move into the adolescent phase of life. Fear drives us. Although we may not actually be in danger of dying, we are programmed to react to anything that shows up as a threat as if our life is in danger. Using the map we have created, we do our best to protect and keep ourselves safe.

This is when we learn to build defenses to hide our weaknesses. We may talk incessantly about senseless things so we don't have to go too deep and feel. We may yell out our anger and our rage to keep things and people at bay when they seem to be getting out of our control. Or we may build an imaginary wall and isolate ourselves so no one can hurt us. People may think we are "rigid" or "cold", but our unconscious motive is to simply keep ourselves safe. We may even "check out" of our bodies when things get too scary. No matter what, we will find ways to protect ourselves from harm and we will do whatever it takes to not get rejected.

We learn strategies to avoid being abandoned. We learn that it's safer to be who and what we think others want us to be. This is the time for us to pull out those masks we created and put them on. We may wear the mask of the "good girl/good boy" who does everything right and never gets anything wrong. Or we may adopt the persona of the perfectionist, the victim or the caretaker. There are thousands of masks to choose from.

If we have parents or caretakers who are able to model for us what an emotionally healthy adult looks like, we quite naturally slide into a healthy adulthood around the age of 25. Unfortunately, only around 3% of us had adults in our life who were that emotionally healthy, who were able to remain present with us as we learned how to process our emotions, who were able to set firm and loving boundaries for and with us, and who demonstrated healthy relationships for us. The other 97% of us were not given the tools to mature into emotionally healthy adults.

This is not the fault of our parents. They weren't given the tools either. And neither were their parents.

So we make do with what we have. We drag the maps and masks of our younger years into adulthood with us. Life is all about surviving and avoiding rejection. It would seem as if we are bound to suffer, no matter what we do. Dysfunctional relationships, addictions, depression, anxiety, codependency, stalled careers, recurring negative patterns: these and many other common maladies have us searching for relief.

What is life like in the Adult Chair?

Life is filled with more peace and happiness. We find ourselves suffering less and less. We experience our own power as we are now armed with tools to help us overcome life's obstacles and issues that arise.

We feel okay with ourselves and begin to like who we are. We have discovered our voice and use it to set boundaries and take care of ourselves.

Many people come to me in my practice or in my workshops and say they want more happiness in their lives. I can see that their experience with happiness mirrors what mine was. That is, happiness comes and goes based on something outside of us.

Think about times when you were happy. The moment you met your true love, the first time you saw a new puppy, the day you bought your first home or a new car. You were flooded with happiness. But after about a month, the newness faded away and you came back to your old "emotional norm." The happiness buzz faded.

We all want happiness that lasts.

The longer I have lived in my Adult Chair, the more I see who I really am. My masks continue to come off. I daily make the choice to be vulnerable and show the world my true self, and I like it! I find that I "own" who I am more and more and am proud of myself. I notice that happiness creeps in far more than ever. Now I'm not saying that I can sustain it all day, every day. But there are no more extreme highs or lows, just a quiet peace. I find that as time goes on, this peace lingers longer and longer. I don't need anything or long for anything to bring me happiness. Peace is more and more my "emotional norm". This inner peace is what I strive for now, regardless of what is happening outside of me.

What is the Adult Chair process like?

This process is not about looking outside yourself for anything or for anyone to validate you. It's about learning how to make yourself strong from the inside out.

During this process of getting to know yourself at your deepest levels, you will discover that you are filled with more goodness and love than you imagined. You will also find that, like every human being, you carry many wounds, most from childhood. We all carry these wounds like bricks in a backpack, zipped up and hidden away. It can be exhausting to lug them around. The effort it takes to keep hidden wounds safely locked up can make us cranky and quick to react, even keep us in a perpetually bad mood, depressed or anxious.

As a therapist, I have learned that we need to look in our past to find these old wounds. As a holistic life coach, I have learned that, to change our life for the better, we need to look to the future and point our attention toward healthy new behaviors and actions. The Adult Chair Model incorporates both past and future.

To live more consistently in our Adult Chair, we will have to learn about the other chairs we have occupied: the Child Chair and the Adolescent Chair. Both have their purposes in our life's journey. Both have their own set of wounds that need to be healed so that we can more easily and frequently be living in the place of our highest selves.

Let us begin.

The Child Chair

"For in every adult there dwells the child that was, and in every child there lies the adult that will be."

John Connolly
The Book of Lost Things (2006)

"Where did my husband and I go wrong?", she asked me. "We gave our children the same Ivy League educations our parents gave us. We've been very successful in our careers. Our kids are successful too. But my eldest daughter is married to an abusive man, my son just married a narcissist, and my youngest is in the middle of a divorce." Her quiet pleading gave away how troubled she really was.

I had literally bumped into this affluent woman when we went to take our seats on the plane. As soon as I had introduced myself and told her what I did, Joanne was asking for my professional opinion. Something had upset her before she got on the plane, and she seemed sincere in her desire to really know where she had gone wrong. So I responded once we were safely airborne.

I asked her how much she and her husband had listened to their children while they were growing up. "Oh, we listened to them alright," she replied emphatically. "And they listened to us." I asked her what she had taught them to do with their emotions. Joanne looked at me with a blank stare and paused, as if I had asked her the most difficult question in the world. Slowly, she replied, "We didn't do emotions. I didn't do emotions. Neither did my husband." She paused. "We really didn't know how to do them with our kids."

It turned out that she and her husband, having both grown up in alcoholic homes, had learned to suppress their emotions and focus entirely on their intellect. The more Joanne talked, the more it sounded to me as if their upbringing had been out of balance, and I told her so. The way she and her husband had been raised—heavy on intellectual intelligence, devoid of emotional intelligence—had left parts of them undeveloped and stunted. Not knowing any other way to parent, they had applied the same approach to their own three children. And now, well, let's say no one was happy with their personal relationships in this family.

I let Joanne know she could get started right away by listening to her daughter without judgment or opinions—and without trying to fix her. This is one of the most powerful things we can do for another human: to listen to them as if there is nothing to fix, as if they are capable of figuring things out on their own. She was excited to get home and give it a try, as she normally offered her daughter solutions, none of which were working.

Joanne was fascinated with the concept of emotional intelligence, my practical tools for working with emotions and the Adult Chair. The rest of the plane ride was taken up with answering her questions. Before we parted ways, this concerned mother of three told me she was eternally grateful for our conversation and that she saw her family in a whole new light.

The Map

Many of the little and big things in the very beginning of our life shape who we become as adults. The purpose of looking back at what shaped us is not to cast blame on those who raised us. Our parents did the best they could with what they knew and who they were. Just as we do the best we can with our children. This is the cycle of life and no one is wrong.

We are looking back to understand our experiences and gain a fresh perspective on them. Now I'm not saying to look back and sit in our experiences. I'm saying look back to gain a better understanding of how they have shaped who we are today.

That said, now let me take you right back to the beginning, just like I did with Joanne. You see I believe trauma starts the moment we are conceived, the very instant the sperm smashes into the egg. From that moment forward, we are picking up on what's going on around us in our environment. Even before we are born, we are recording everything, including how people are relating to us, without discernment.

Were you wanted? Were you planned? Were you a mistake? Were you adopted? Were your parents thrilled about you?

Did your parents fight when you were in utero? Were you in intensive care when you were born? How often did people touch or hold you as a baby?

During our early development, life is all about learning. This is when we are firmly seated in our Child Chair. We are learning about our feelings and needs, creativity and fun, trust and passion. We are learning about our vulnerability and intimacy. We are learning what works and what doesn't. And by about the age of seven, we start relating to what we have learned as our "map".

Key Learnings

One of the most important things we learn while we are in our Child Chair has to do with our "true" feelings and "true" needs. We figure out whether it's safe to express those feelings and how to get our needs met. This becomes the "roadmap" for how we navigate through the world.

What do I mean by True Feelings? Many people I work with assume True Feelings are the obvious two: love and anger. Actually, we have a full spectrum of feelings that range from love to fear. During our early development as children, we learn and experience all of these beautiful emotions. We learn about love and anger, sadness and joy, excitement and despair, bliss and frustration. The list goes on and on.

When we experience our feelings and express them truthfully, it can be uncomfortable for our caregivers. Sometimes they don't know what to do with the power of these emotions. When they want us to stop expressing what we are feeling, we translate that into what I call "faulty programming".

If you were loved and embraced when you were hurt, you probably learned that vulnerability and touch are safe and good.

But if you were yelled at for crying or punished for showing emotions, you probably learned to hide your sadness and excitement. You may even have felt unsafe or even ashamed of these parts of yourself. As young children, many of us begin to push down emotions that adults tell us we are not "supposed" to feel. We learn to block those feelings from coming up and to only allow ourselves to let the ones that we are not punished for show.

Now let's take a look at our True Needs. A true need is not what we want, but what we actually need. This can be anything from food, water and shelter to a hug and someone saying "I love you." In the first few years of our life, we discover what these basic needs are and experience having them met and not having them met.

Did you hear, "I love you..." when you were growing up? How often were you hugged? Did people touch you in appropriately loving ways when you needed comfort? Were your caregivers attentive and able to meet all your needs?

This is not always the case. For the first nine months of my life, I had colic and cried for 20 hours a day. My mother had to take Valium to deal with my crying. I can appreciate what she went through: when my own children were young and cried for more than 20 minutes, it completely stressed me out. I can't imagine being with a crying baby hours upon hours a day! My mother told me there were times when she just couldn't take it and would "let me cry" in my crib. I don't recall the first few months of my life but, if I had to hazard a guess, I would say my needs weren't met. Over and over again, I would have been in pain and truly needed someone to hold me or take my pain away, but no one came.

If we are not asked about our needs, if we are told that they don't matter or are made to feel ashamed of them during our childhood, we tend to take that part of ourselves and tuck it away. We hide our true needs and figure out other ways to cope or get them met. For instance, I developed a way to cope when my mother didn't come when I was crying. It was brilliantly simple (as any strategy developed by a child is): don't count on others and definitely don't lean on anyone. Take care of yourself and be strong. That became part of my unconscious road map. It wasn't until I sat in my Adult Chair that I realized this part of my map needed updating.

Now think back to your childhood.

Were you allowed to feel all of your feelings? Did you have to take care of someone else's feelings and ignore your own? Were you shamed for feeling what you felt? Or did someone sit with you and be with you in that feeling and help guide you out of it?

Perhaps you grew up in an alcoholic, abusive or even violent home. So you learned a safe way to survive: keep yourself emotionless so you don't upset anyone or rock the boat. Or perhaps you grew up in a home where your caregivers pushed you to be smart and educated so they would be happy. So you learned an intelligent way to survive: focus on your intellect and push your emotions away.

What kind of map did you write to help you navigate your early life? What parts of your inner child went into hiding? Do these parts come out at all today?

Around the age of seven, we slide from our Child Chair and into our Adolescent Chair. We hand over all our childhood learnings and experiences, along with our maps, to our adolescent self. It is time for us to become individuals. Now it is the ego's job to take over and keep us safe and alive.

In The Child Chair

- Innocence
- True Feelings & True Needs
- Creativity
- Passion
- Fun
- Spontaneity
- Trust
- Vulnerability
- Intimacy

The Adolescent Chair

"Adolescence is the conjugator of childhood and adulthood."

Louise J. Kaplan
Adolescence: The Farewell to Childhood (1984)

As a child, I was painfully shy and hardly spoke to anyone, except my two closest friends and family. I remember one day back in fourth grade, I was very upset with something my gym teacher had said. As he turned his back to our group, I flipped him off. The kids all around me were roaring with laughter. That laughter felt like positive reinforcement in the moment. And that moment marked the start of my process of becoming an individual, the very beginning of my journey to figure out who I was and how I fit in the world.

I began to do more things that were out of line to find out what made kids laugh. The attention I got for acting up felt so good to my ego. Every laugh validated me. So I kept doing things that were out of line. Suddenly, I had all kinds of friends who thought I was funny. I became known as the girl who was willing to try anything to get attention.

The beginning of the move into your Adolescent Chair happens when you realize that "I" exist separate from the "we" of your family (and the world). With the arrival of the ego, comes the awareness that the world is unsafe. The ego is based in fear and its job is to keep us alive.

The Adolescent Chair is the seat of the survivor. Everything here is focused on helping us survive. The energy in this chair is faster. It's on guard and needs to stay alert. Like a relay runner, the ego takes everything the child has collected and recorded, including inner programming and strategies, and runs with it.

There's an incredible sense of urgency to life now. There is the past and the future to keep an eye on. Everything is black and white. There is no time in the present to deal with the feelings and needs of our now "inner" child, so he/she gets cast aside. You have to run your own life!

And so the ego does its best. It follows the child's roadmap and develops more tactics along the way to keep you alive and free from physical and emotional pain.

One tactic is to cast aside those childhood feelings and needs. No room or time to feel emotions when you're developing survival strategies.

Another tactic is to adopt a persona. We may become perfectionists or slobs, cold and uncaring addicts or rescuing co-dependents. We may blame others for our misfortune and get stuck in a victim mentality. Whatever personas we adopt, we feel pressured to make decisions and to do things RIGHT NOW, and so we either rush in or we resist rushing and procrastinate. Either way, we don't believe we have time to think things through if we're going to stay safe and alive. Better to rely on the programming we inherited from our child.

Yet another tactic is to use masks like the one I did. Masks cover up our true self so we will be accepted, rather than judged, rejected or abandoned.

The Masks

Do you change who you are in order to fit in at work? Do you ever dress a certain way to please others or to fit in? Do you act a certain way around certain people?

How do you show up with your friends? Do you bite your tongue so you don't piss anyone off? Who do you become around your family so they will love you?

Every mask begins when someone approves of you being inauthentic.

Most of us lose our true selves at some point in childhood. We take on a belief that who we are isn't good enough to be loved and accepted. So we change ourselves for others, hoping not to be rejected. Every time we change who we are for another, every time we show up as someone we are not, we are putting on a mask.

We can make ourselves look any way we think we need to be in order to protect our true self and avoid rejection. We can be defensive and argumentative or timid and quiet. Our ego will come up with any mask it can in order to protect itself. There are hundreds to choose from. We choose whichever mask we believe will work.

Think back to your adolescent years.

How were you treated? What were the spoken and unspoken messages you got from your caregivers about how you should be?

Now think of how you change yourself today to attempt to gain other people's approval or acceptance.

Which mask do you wear most often? And what does that look like?

Perhaps you are getting ready to divorce your spouse. You are plagued with overwhelming sadness and grief, yet you put on the mask of serenity and act as if everything is fine. Or perhaps you're really feeling lonely and depressed. But you smile through it all, letting your friends know that "Life is great!"

I kept using my "living on the edge" mask well into my 20s. It wasn't until I began learning about self-awareness that I decided that maybe being the one who is so extreme just for laughs wasn't such a good idea anymore.

To take a mask down, we must discover what it covers up. When we can expose the part of ourselves that we are hiding and get to know it, we can be free of that mask. The key lies in looking at what's underneath. Revealing the true self sets us free.

Key Learnings

In the Adolescent Chair, we do not know what to do with what we are feeling, especially our pain. In fact, when we experience a negative emotion, it causes distress in our system, since it pulls attention away from surviving.

Here is where we first encounter triggers. A trigger is like a button that gets pushed when someone or something connects with an emotion that we have hidden (or are unaware of). For example, my feelings around not being important or not being accepted might get triggered when all my friends get invited to a party but me, or when I really like someone and find out they don't like me back.

What do you do when you feel pain or stress? What do you do when you get triggered?

We all learn ways to calm and numb our pain. Many of us create vices: we reach for the drink or the pill, the joystick or the remote control. We live in anticipation of the cocktail or the exciting new experience that we think will bring us happiness. But the "happiness buzz" doesn't last. So we try to solve the problem by losing weight or gaining weight, by getting a new boyfriend or getting married, by having kids or having the perfect home.

What's really happening is that we're putting temporary bandages on top of unhealed pain.

There is no way to get through life without being hurt. Yet we all do our best to cover up our wounds so no one can see them. We believe our wounded parts are bad, broken and unlovable. This is simply not true.

When in our Adolescent Chair, we are navigating the world with the emotional intelligence of a twelve-year-old. The strategies we come up with for dealing with emotional pain, stress and triggers at that age have to do with things like shopping, eating cake, gaming or drinking.

This may sound as if the Adolescent Chair is a bad place. It is not. It only feels like a bad place when we think we're stuck here and believe we have no alternatives.

In fact, we need this chair and cannot exist without it. This is where we connect with not only our ego, but also the logical part of our mind, the left brain part of us that dials the phone, tells us to stop at the stop sign, and directs us onto the right turnoff when we're driving down the expressway. We need our ego and our logic to survive in the world as an individual. Without them, we could not function.

To get ourselves unstuck, we need to bring in a third party— our healthy adult. Our adult can bring our child together with our adolescent and create a peaceful way for them to co-exist. This is the secret to the three chairs.

When we are in our Adult Chair, we are bringing consciousness into this triad. Only a healthy adult can be with a child and all of their feelings and needs and, at the same time, be with an adolescent with all the thoughts and ideas coming from their ego and then bring all those feelings, needs, thoughts and ideas together. Just like an amazing CEO in an executive meeting, our adult is in charge. Our adult brings "executive powers" to the problems we have to solve and the decisions we have to make: our adult brings consciousness, intuition, connection, compassion and clear thinking to our life.

Only our adult can do this.

Only our adult will ever ask about our True Feelings and Needs and make sure they are taken care of. Only our adult can show the adolescent the triggers, masks and personas they have adopted. Unfortunately, many of us never get a chance to meet our adult. We get lost searching outside ourselves for the person, place or thing that will create this inner balance for us.

My adult was the part of myself that I was missing and that I found. But I didn't find it by searching outside. I found it by traveling inside. Let me show you how to get started on this inward journey and what it's like to sit in the third chair.

Time now to slide over into the Adult Chair and grow yourself up.

In The Adolescent Chair

- Urgency ("I must do this right NOW!")
- Ego
- Unconscious
- Absolutes & Extremes
- Personas: Survivor, Rescuer, Perfectionist, Victim, Blamer, Co-dependent, Enabler, Love Addict, Love Avoidant, Addict, Judge, Critic, etc.
- Blaming Others
- Living in the Past & the Future
- Making up Stories & Assumptions
- Creating and Wearing Masks

The Adult Chair

*"As a child I assumed that when I reached adulthood, I
would have grown-up thoughts."*

David Sedaris
Let's Explore Diabetes with Owls (2014)

Welcome to your Adult Chair. Here you are fully present,
empowered and authentic. Here you can observe your
adolescent and your inner child and help them work together,
with you as their adult guide.

Sound too good to be true?

Well, it's true. What it looks like, though, is probably
different from what you're thinking.

I'll be honest with you. You are not going to wake up one
day in your Adult Chair and suddenly have this magical life.

You can, however, incorporate the Adult Chair into your life bit by bit until one day you live in it more than you do now. As you learn how to access this framework for loving yourself more and more, other relationships may change. In some cases, this can look a bit miraculous.

Laura was attending one of my eight-week Adult Chair Intensives a couple of years ago. She shared with us at the beginning of the program that she was in an unhealthy marriage. She made a promise that she would try sitting in her Adult Chair more often, focusing on facts and on living in the present moment as much as she could. She also did her best to not believe stories her ego was telling her so she could avoid getting pulled into her Adolescent Chair.

Toward the end of our sessions, she came in and reported to us that she was speaking up for herself to her verbally condescending husband and holding her power. When we begin to love ourselves, our innate ability to stand up for ourselves gets activated. It's natural for us to stop putting up with being stepped on, used or treated unkindly. Some relationships will change to allow us to be our authentic, healed self: others may not survive.

In Laura's case, by practicing just a few key concepts of the Adult Chair, she had begun to love herself and realize she was worthy of respect. With that realization came her voice and an ability to set healthier boundaries in her marriage. She was shocked at herself—and thrilled at the shift in her relationship with her husband—as were we! I remember we actually all cheered for her.

The Adult Chair is, essentially, where we achieve self-realization. This is where we learn about all of our parts and listen to all of the voices in our heads, where we get to know them so well that we can identify what chair we are in at any given moment and then CHOOSE to slide into our adult.

This is where you will learn who you really are, what hurts, what feels broken, what scares you, where you find passion and happiness as a grown-up, and what it will take to be at peace with all of it. This is where you heal.

According to Bruce Lipton, stem cell biologist and epigeneticist, we rarely live "in consciousness." Most of us live unconsciously, in routines, with little idea how to get out of our ruts. This also means we live from a reactionary place, a place where we make quick judgements and fast decisions and do anything we can to stay safe. Living from this place can be exhausting.

Moving into your Adult Chair changes all this. Bruce Lipton says that living here, in consciousness, even just 10% of each day can send ripples of change through your life. It has changed my life. And I know it has changed the lives of countless others.

I invite you to start with that goal in mind.

The Observer

Eckhart Tolle and many spiritual teachers speak of the power of stepping outside of your life and living life as the observer. This is something we can only do from our Adult Chair. When we observe and become the "watcher" of our lives, we remain conscious. Everything slows down. We can respond, instead of react, to what's happening.

In our Adult Chair, we observe what we are feeling and thinking. We see our Adolescent Chair and our Child Chair. We notice what is going on in the moment, we become aware of our emotions and needs, we process them (instead of reacting impulsively), and then express ourselves. We respond, rather than react, to life.

In the Adult Chair, we are patient. We can wait. We can make new choices that both protect us and get our needs met. We become empowered.

The longer I can sit in my Adult Chair, the more I can observe, the more I can let go, the more I can be at peace.

In the Adult Chair, we are in the seat of consciousness. We are connected to the "bigger" part of ourselves, as well as being firmly grounded in the moment. So when we are "triggered" by circumstances or people and an uncomfortable emotion comes up, we can observe ourselves and recognize what has activated us. Being triggered is actually a healing opportunity.

Triggers come from our "shadow self", that part of ourselves that we feel we must hide from the world. The next time you get triggered, use the opportunity to bring the light of your consciousness to what is hidden in the shadows. The world is our mirror: we can choose to look at our reflection or look away until another time. There are very few times when someone says something to us that isn't ours. So instead of getting mad at the person who sparked your upset, instead of shutting them down or blaming them, take a look in the mirror.

What is this person trying to show me about myself?

I encourage you to look inside and learn more about yourself. See your old wounds, the ones that you don't want anyone else to see or know about, for what they are. Bring them into the light, own them as parts of yourself and accept that there is no reason to hide them anymore. Know that, as you begin to identify your main triggers, the ones that keep coming up again and again, you can work through them alone or find someone to help.

Eventually, they will come up less and less.

Key Learnings

We must get to know ourselves so well that we can see where we are coming from.

When I began this process, I realized I would have to get to know what lit up my inner child, as well as what her feelings and needs were. I would also have to get to know which persona was taking the seat in my Adolescent Chair in any particular moment. Was it my inner critic, the blamer, the analytic, the perfectionist or the victim? Once I discovered that, I could then slide into my Adult Chair and become the compassionate observer of it all, patiently disengage (not disassociate) from any story or upset I had about what was going on, and make some new choices for myself.

My life has changed completely since learning about my Adult Chair. I used to have emotional highs and lows, bouts of depression and anxiety. Now I have a framework for understanding and loving myself. Now I have the experience of living authentically from my truth, instead of from stories and assumptions. Much more now, I am the "watcher", the observer of my life. And that helps me stay in my power.

Best of all, I have found what I was looking for all along: inner peace. When sitting in the Adult Chair, there is a calmness that sweeps over you. Everything seems to slow down and you find yourself slipping into the present moment and gaining clarity. Everything suddenly feels like it's going to be OK, no matter what the circumstances are. There is a trust in life that I have never experienced before, a new faith that everything is exactly as it is supposed to be. This place of stability, empowerment and truth is not something we can prepare for intellectually.

Here you can feel your emotions fully and know what to do when you are triggered. You can discover your needs and get them met. If you are struggling with an addiction or a vice, you are able to become aware of it and make conscious changes. Your relationships change. You live a more stable life.

The Adult Chair brings you back home to your true self. This is where you experience the highest version of yourself in human form.

Welcome home.

In The Adult Chair

- Seat of Consciousness

- The Observer

- Living in the Present Moment

- Focus on Facts & Truth

- Compassion & Patience

- Boundaries

- Empowerment

Living in The Adult Chair

"*When we graduate from childhood into adulthood, we're thrown into this confusing, Cthulhu-like miasma of life, filled with social and career problems, all with branching choices and no correct answers.*"

Felicia Day
You're Never Weird on the Internet (2015)

So how do we do this Adult Chair thing? Are you overwhelmed yet? Excited about taking responsibility for who you are? Ready to put more energy into sitting in your Adult Chair but have no clue how?

Well, here are eight tips to get you started. Use them to get some experience with how easy it is to slide into your own Adult Chair.

1. IT'S ALL ABOUT ME! Get comfortable with putting yourself first.

I preach this to my clients. Some respond with a horrified look, "But I am not a selfish person. I can't do that."

Putting yourself first is not about being selfish. Putting yourself first is living with a focus on yourself first. Living with a focus on yourself is about self-awareness, not selfishness.

You want to know when you are emotionally off or triggered, physically in pain, wearing a mask, stuck in codependency, or reacting and reaching for a vice. You want to know yourself so well that you can see when you are making unconscious choices (like overeating or binge drinking) and catch yourself so you can make a new empowered choice.

You want to be more mindful. Because if you are not focused on yourself and what's going on within you, then you must be focused on someone else. If you are focused outside yourself, you can miss what's really going on with you and end up blaming someone else.

"It's all about me" is also an act of love.

If you still hesitate to switch to this focus, remember that when the plane is going down, the best thing you can do – for everyone's sake – is give yourself oxygen first, then your partner, your kids and your friends. Same thing applies here.

When you are taking care of yourself first, everyone around you benefits.

2. OBSERVE YOUR LIFE Many people ask me how to become an observer of their life. I suggest they think of it like this.

When you get triggered or find yourself getting emotional about something, take yourself out of it. See what's happening in your life as if it's a story being played out on a stage—and you're sitting in the audience watching the whole show.

This shift in perspective changes everything. It disassociates you from the event so you can gain a new—and higher— perspective on what's going on. It lowers your emotional reaction to the situation. And it also helps you more clearly see options and choices that you couldn't see when you were stuck in the "drama" of the play.

3. BECOME A STORY BUSTER My friend Catherine was beside herself. Her daughter had just been placed in a college dorm in a basement. She was upset because she "knew" her daughter would absolutely hate it: she would get sick all the time from the drafts and it was close to a party area so it would be loud and she wouldn't be able to study. She would not do well in school. Catherine went on and on about how bad her daughter's experience was going to be because of her dorm placement.

My friend lived with anxiety and angst for a month before her daughter left for college. She had made up a story about what she thought her daughter's experience was going to be like—and lived with it as if it was the truth.

Two weeks into the first semester, I asked how her daughter was doing. Catherine replied as calmly as she could that her daughter loved her dorm room: it was whisper quiet, perfect for studying, cool in hot weather and warm in cold. Her daughter couldn't be happier.

Like many of us, Catherine had been wrong! She had needlessly spent a whole month in emotional turmoil. All that angst could have been over immediately if she had decided to find out what the facts were and "bust that story".

Fact #1: her daughter was going to college. Fact #2: her daughter had been placed in the basement level of the dorms. And that's all the facts!

All it takes to become a Story Buster is to stay present in a balanced emotional state to what's happening in our lives. Practice focusing on what is fact and truth **in this moment.** Be conscious and mindful about what you are saying to yourself and what you are saying out loud. Look at what you know to be 100% true about the situation you are in. Doing this blows up any assumptions and stories your adolescent may have created about what's happening.

This is another way to maintain peace in our lives. Now who doesn't need more of that?

4. CONNECT WITH YOUR INNER CHILD Just

because we are adults doesn't mean we don't possess a very real, very innocent and vulnerable part of us that is tucked deep inside experiencing very real feelings and needs. This part is what we call the "inner child". Connecting with our inner child, reconnects us to our True Feelings and Needs and opens the door to experience a new aliveness and wholeness that we didn't know was possible.

How do we access this child within? One way is to begin to "check in" with him/her. Simply ask, "How do I feel?" or "How does this make me feel?" As you do this, imagine yourself as a small child sitting in front of you. The idea here is to simply observe what emotion you are feeling without judging it.

By asking in this way, we activate aspects of both the Child Chair and the Adult Chair at the same time. Only the adult would ever ask this question and listen to what the child has to say. Fortunately, the more time we spend connecting with our child, the more we activate our adult.

Knowing what we truly feel can change us in profound and simple ways. After practicing connecting with my inner child for a short time, I found myself asking my sons if they wanted to go rollerblading with me. They were in shock! I had fallen terribly on roller blades years before and sworn I'd never skate again. I was truly afraid to get on them. But to my inner child rollerblading still sounded like so much FUN! Experiencing fun and spontaneity are sure signs that you have connected with your inner child.

Anticipate new aspects of yourself showing up that have been hidden when you begin to do this work. You never know what will show up next.

5. LEARN TO BREATHE Many of us fear feeling. What we actually fear is not the feeling itself, but the idea that we will get stuck in that emotion. When a particularly strong emotion begins to rise up within us, the Adolescent/Ego will often see that as a threat to our existence and will try to shut it down. The goal here is to not push away what you are feeling, but to bring it up, let it come through and then let it go.

When a client comes in and reports "feeling stuck", I help them go into what their body is feeling and the emotion hidden inside. This helps release what's stuck and allows it to move through the body. Deep breathing is great to get emotions to slide all the way through.

Most of us don't breathe well or correctly. Our breathing is usually shallow and quick, and we often hold it. Short, shallow breathing activates our sympathetic nervous system, the fight-or-flight response that kicks into action when we are being chased by a lion. This releases cortisol into the bloodstream and taxes our adrenals. Many of us are walking around in permanent stress response and we don't even know it because this way of breathing has become our norm!

On a daily basis, breathing deeply is the way to go. Deep, conscious breathing activates the relaxation response. It triggers the parasympathetic nervous system, releasing endorphins that help us sleep, lower our blood pressure, improve our immune function and counter ruminating thoughts that lead to anxiety and depression. The best part about breathing deeply and slowing down is that it puts us in our Adult Chair, where we can recognize our feelings, think clearly and make wise choices about what's best for us.

The Belly Breath is an easy-to-learn technique to help you relax, slow down and step into the present moment. Place your hand on your belly button and inhale deeply and slowly to a count of four, extending the belly out as far as it can go. Gently push your belly out as you keep inhaling: you can go farther than you think you can. Hold for four counts. Then exhale slowly to a count of four, slowly bringing your belly back in. Again, contract your belly farther than you think you can. At the completion of this exhale, hold for four counts. This completes one cycle of the Belly Breath.

PS. Crying cleanses the soul, so go for it if it feels right!

6. GROUNDING When we are grounded, we feel centered, calm and clear. We are fully alive in the moment. Sound like the Adult Chair? When we are in the Adult Chair, we are grounded!

But what is it to be grounded? We hear this word often but few of us know what it actually means. To be grounded means your "energetic body" (or aura) is attached to the earth. That energetic body surrounds your physical body.

Stepping outside in bare feet, leaning against a tree or contemplating a sunset for 10 to 15 minutes are simple ways to ground yourself. Even taking a slow, deep breath can bring you back into the moment and can be beneficial for grounding. A guided grounding meditation is another one of my favorite ways to get connected to the earth. There are countless others. Experiment and find what makes you feel grounded.

7. MEDITATION Why meditation? It helps the mind slow down and the nervous system quiet down. It also helps us relax so we can more easily slide into the present moment and, yes, into our Adult Chair.

Many people tell me they can't meditate. They don't have time. Or they can't quiet their minds. Personally, I am a fan of guided meditations, especially short ones. They are a quick and easy way to access the "adult state". That is why I have created a series of short meditations—anywhere from one to ten minutes long—and posted them on my website and YouTube channel. They can help you with slowing down and stepping into the present moment, cleansing negative emotions, freeing yourself of stress, loving yourself, finding your inner child, and getting yourself grounded. They're all free, so take a minute to check them out in the Resources section at the back of this book.

Remember, you don't have to be sitting cross-legged on a meditation cushion to do this. Meditation can happen during a walk, during a drive or while you're just sitting quietly in a chair. There are countless ways to meditate and I encourage you to find one that works for you.

8. CALL IN YOUR ADULT When everything seems to be going down the drain and your feelings are out of control, call in your adult. Simply say to yourself out loud, "I need my adult NOW!" Then wait…and notice what happens next.

Become sensitive to the slightest shift in your energy. Pay close attention to what you are aware of and what you intuitively "know". Whatever you notice may be barely perceptible in the beginning. But as your higher self begins to enter the picture more and more often, you'll become more aware, more attuned to how life is unfolding around you and through you. You'll experience more balance and more insights than you thought possible. With your adult's help, you can experience more love—both for yourself and others—in your life.

What's Next?

"My mother had breast cancer. My sister had breast cancer. And now I've got it. Obviously, there's a pattern in our family. I want you to help me learn how to process my emotions differently."

Those were the first words I heard Connie say in our initial one-on-one session.

So I shared the three chairs with her and how the Adult Chair Model came to be (you can read about it in My Story at the end of this book). Then I helped her connect with her inner child and her inner adolescent to form relationships with them both. Whenever her mind began making up worst case scenarios, we would get her adult to observe what was going on and reel her scared child and adolescent back in to calm. She got in touch with her true feelings, as well as her true needs. Instead of covering up or numbing her pain with alcohol, food, TV or some other vice, she journaled, talked to and cried with her inner child.

Connie started making choices about her care and her support that worked *for her*—instead of just blindly following what everyone expected her to choose. She stopped going to support groups because they only made her feel worse. She asked the nurses and doctors to stop telling her what to expect because that made her more scared. She instead focused on being present in the moment, noticing what pain or emotion was coming up, if any, and staying with it. She learned to be more centered and present in her body, to concentrate more on positive thoughts and visualizations about her immune system, and to establish boundaries around what she needed and wanted.

Connie went through breast cancer with the three chairs—and she had a very different experience than most people do with a similar diagnosis. She was able to very gracefully do "life with cancer". She told me, "The Adult Chair helped me feel like I wasn't just thrown to the wolves. It gave me a way to be in my body and in balance." I can't tell you what an honor and a gift it has been for me to walk with her in this part of her life's journey.

You may not have to deal with cancer in this lifetime. But we all will have difficult times, times when we need other ideas and people and tools to help us. What matters is what you choose to do where your time of difficulty arrives.

What's next then is entirely up to you. My hope is that you, like Connie, will have the courage to learn how to sit more and more consistently in your Adult Chair.

Life changes in ways we can't even imagine—but only when we get to know and love all of our*selves*.

Here's looking at all of you...

Resources

If you're interested in exploring this work in more detail or in learning how to sit in your Adult Chair more consistently, check out these possibilities on my website, iTunes, and YouTube channels.

The Adult Chair Podcast

(http://theadultchair.com)
Catch our weekly conversations about stress, anxiety, depression, physical health, self-love, peace and emotional balance, and how our understanding of ourselves impacts the most important relationships in our lives.

The Adult Chair Private Facebook Group

(https://www.facebook.com/groups/theadultchair)
I've created a private group on Facebook for the brave people who are ready to live in the healthiest version of themselves: The Adult Chair. It's a safe-space, a members-only area designed to share vulnerability, to take off masks and show the world who we really are. We're all learning to find our inner voices and in this private group, we have a place to practice with encouragement, patience, support, and love.

Individual Sessions

(http://michellechalfant.com/individual)
Find and learn how to live consistently in your healthy and authentic Adult Chair. This process of discovery and adaptation blends traditional counseling with life coaching and alternative healing techniques.

Couples Sessions

(http://michellechalfant.com/couples)

Learn how to operate in your primary relationship from your Adult Chair. Discover how to be mindful, conscious and authentic with your mate."

Workshops

(http://michellechalfant.com/workshops)
Come join me at one of our upcoming sessions and experience your life transformed!

Meditations

(http://michellechalfant.com/meditations)
No time to meditate? No more excuses! Listen to my library of 1, 5, 10-minute and longer guided meditations, all free on the website to listen or download.

YouTube

(http://www.youtube.com/MichelleChalfant)
All my podcasts and meditations in one place. Subscribe to my channel and you'll be notified whenever I post anything new.

Instagram

(https://www.instagram.com/michelle.chalfant/)

Michelle's Story

I grew up in an Italian family in upstate New York. My childhood was typical (or so I thought) of ethnic families. There were no individual boundaries, just "the family". Family included my father and mother, my younger sister and me, my aunts and uncles, my cousins, and my grandmother, "Queenie" Carmella.

The whole family spent LOTS of time together. There were weekends, Sunday dinners, all the sporting events we kids were involved in and, of course, entire summers spent together in the big house on the lake.

Some of my best memories come from those summers at the lake – and some of my worst. Alcohol was a "family" staple. I never saw anyone after 4 p.m. without a cocktail in their hands. In fact, I still remember asking my father when I would like the taste of alcohol. The adults laughed at me, but I was very serious. Didn't they expect me to drink alcohol someday? I thought this was something all adults did.

My father and his identical twin brother were like one person, only my father was the most loving man I have ever encountered and his brother the most angry. My uncle was jealous of us and anyone that took my father's time. He could ruin a Sunday meal, and then no one would talk about it the next day. I hated liars and sweeping things under the rug. I wanted to speak truth. I wanted others to do so as well.

I remember feeling the pain my father was in, always wanting us to all be together as one big happy family. But it was like having a giant thorn in with a bunch of balloons. It just couldn't work. Mix in the alcohol and, boy, you can imagine the fights and issues we had.

I could feel my mother's sadness with never being able to be number one with my father. I could sense the stress all this put on my parent's marriage. Around age six, I took it upon myself to begin taking care of my mother. By twelve, I felt like I had to protect my mom from my uncle's verbal abuse (my father, caught in the middle, would say nothing). Of course, I had to take my younger sister under my wing as well and be strong enough for them both. My longing to fix everyone, combined with my innate ability to problem solve, turned this into full-blown codependency.

During my teens, I unconsciously looked for ways to numb out. Alcohol and other things helped. So did helping everyone who had issues. I also found myself flipping between longing for love in a partnership and avoiding it entirely. I wanted my boyfriends to save me, to take me away from my pain. When I'd get a boyfriend, I'd put a wall up and, at the same time, I wouldn't want them to leave. I couldn't risk getting enmeshed with another person. After all, I already had my sister and mother to fend for. I later learned that I was caught between love addiction and love avoidance.

By my early 20s, I knew something was wrong. I went to a psychiatrist and asked him why I would spontaneously begin crying. He told me I was depressed and sent me out the door with a prescription for Prozac. I remember wondering why he didn't want to hear my story. Taking meds felt wrong, but I had no other option. I tried Prozac for a week and it made me feel awful. I stopped.

In my family, I was told, "we don't air our dirty laundry" to strangers. There was no Internet back then, no Google, no therapist on every corner to turn to. So I was forced to read to find some answers as to why I felt this self-hatred and loneliness.

Everything kept pointing towards one thing: I had to love myself.

Great. Well, how the hell do I do that?

As many others before had done, I became a therapist to find out how to heal my own issues. I got a degree in Psychology, a masters in Rehabilitation Counseling, and a license in counseling.

Traditional counseling was good, but I wanted more. So I delved into what I was personally curious and passionate about: spirituality and "non-traditional" healing modalities. I studied spiritual texts, yoga, meditation, the energy bodies, and the meridian system that acupuncturists use. I integrated these non-traditional modalities into my therapeutic practice. Interestingly, my clients were looking for help with the very things that I longed for.

But self-defeating thoughts still plagued me and left me exhausted and sad. So I intensified my search for a deeper understanding of self and self-love.

Along the way, I studied with some of the best teachers out there: Debbie Ford, Byron Katie, Pia Mellody, Abraham–Hicks, Gary Craig, Alan Cohen, Dr. Wayne Dyer, Tony Robbins and many others who were top in their field. If I couldn't see them live, I'd watch them and read everything they put out. I began to see some common links to self-love. Over the years, I slowly started to make sense of the lack of self-love and what to do about it.

It wasn't until I moved to Nashville that everything really came together. Well-known teacher Susan Austin-Crumpton introduced me to her concept of the self, as expressed through three chairs. I had worked with other experiential therapies like Gestalt that used chairs, but I loved the simplicity of Susan's work and her version of the Adult, Adolescent and Child Chairs. With her blessing, I integrated what I learned during four years of intense study with her with everything I had learned so far in my own pilgrimage of self-love to create *The Adult Chair Model.*

We invite you to share this book with others! Please forward MichelleChalfant.com to friends, family, and colleagues where they can learn about the book and buy their own copy.

For volume purchases, contact us at MichelleChalfant.com.

Thank you.

Made in the USA
Middletown, DE
27 November 2018